WILD SONGS

JOY LOVE and LOSS

SAM MCMICHAEL

DEDICATION

This work is dedicated to the increase of loving-kindness, the appreciation of joy, and the cultivation of equanimity.

ACKNOWLEDGMENTS

Thanks to Terry Gresham for his inspiration, encouragement, and technical assistance. Thanks to Terree McMichael for her magnificent cover design, illustrations, and for always being my first and most insightful critic. Thanks to Carla Winters for her unflagging enthusiasm, constant encouragement, and invaluable technical assistance. Thanks to John Morris for his critique of the sonnet cycle and his appreciation of my poetic efforts. Thanks to the many friends and fellow poets who have helped keep the poetic spark alive over the years.

INTRODUCTION

Though never my student, Sam McMichael is an alumnus of Cameron University where I teach. I know him primarily because of his regular participation over many years in a monthly open coffeehouse reading under the aegis of the Cameron Beta Omicron chapter of Sigma Tau Delta, the English honor society, that has been offered in various venues in Lawton since January of 1996; I serve as its emcee. Since 2007, the home for that reading has been the Unitarian Universalist Church in Lawton, a church of which Sam, who resides in Apache, is one of the leading parishioners; he generously offered the church as a venue when participants were hampered by having to read over the clatter of plates and coffee machine in the center of a noisy local restaurant, and he drives into town on the third Saturday of every month to open the church for students and members of the greater Lawton-Ft. Sill community who bring their work to read. As one of the event's vital participants, he also brings his work, and I always look forward to what I have come to regard as the gospel according to Sam.

Sam is a storyteller, philosopher, spiritualist, and poet all rolled into one man, and *Wild Songs* reveals each of these facets. These poems—some of them abstract philosophical forays into the big ideas about life, time, love, survival, and salvation and some of them concrete etudes of the natural world and its "brute facts"—reveal a lifelong spiritual seeker, thinker, and reader of such poetic masters as Frost, Yeats, Eliot, Thomas, Brooks, Stevens, Cummings, and Pinsky, all of whom are either explicitly alluded to or implicitly invoked in these pages. Sam explores a range of poetic form from free verse to acrostics to received European forms such as the sonnet and villanelle all the way up to his audacious attempt at what Gregory Corso in his *Book of Forms* identifies as the Italian heroic crown of fifteen sonnets, entitled "It's About Time." As the title of his heroic crown suggests, Sam is serious and playful at the same time, never taking himself too seriously; in a good example, the speaker of "Pinsky's Definition" arrives at an amusingly self-deprecating conclusion: "I know I would not want / My final resting place to be / On page 493 of a Norton anthology. / Perhaps I needn't worry." Such sprightly thought and music deserve your full attention; it will always have mine. Enjoy.

Dr. John Graves Morris: Professor of English at Cameron University, Author of *Noise and Stories.*

CONTENTS

PART I

PART II

PART III

PART IV

PART I

SUBMERGED IN SHADOW

Sit submerged in shadow
Beneath the bending trees
Watch sunlight fall in patches
Through the trembling leaves
Still the clamor of the heart
Put away the questing mind
Learn all that man can know
Of timelessness and time

JOY, LOVE, AND LOSS

I.

An old man walked out one dew drenched, moon drenched,
Pre-dawn, early summer morning,
To drink his first cup of coffee and open himself
To the ten directions.
As he sat sipping in silence, he heard a rush of wings
As mockingbird swam through the moon-lit air,
Found the tip of the tallest near-by tree
And settled there.
Mockingbird fluttered her wings, stretched her neck,
And began to sing.
With every liquid note she sang
Joy joy joy
Love
And loss loss loss
This fluid moment is now forever lost.

II.

The old man sat, sipping coffee and listening to
Bird song
As the day began to dawn.
A sliver of light penetrated the chicken coop
And struck the eye of the Dominicker rooster.
Rooster ruffled his wings, stretched his neck
And began to shout,
And with every raucous, discordant shout, he shouted
Awake
Awake to joy joy joy
Love
And loss loss loss
This moment of awakening is now forever lost

5.

III.

Still the old man sat, and still he sipped.
As the world began to awake around him
The eastern horizon continued to fall away
Revealing more and more sun-lit sky
Washing away the moon-lit night.
Old man coyote, returning to the hills
From his night's hunt in the flats,
Paused, pointed his nose to the sky
And gave out a wavering, quavering howl,
And with every howl he howled out
Joy joy joy
Love
And loss loss loss
This moment of returning is now forever lost.

IV.

As the echoes of the howls died away in the canyons,
A flock of crows rose from a chinaberry grove
And circled higher and higher
And as they rose they circled wider and wider
Cawing out to the world and to one another
And with every caw they cawed out
Joy joy joy
Love
And loss loss loss
This rising moment is now forever lost.

V.

That old man emptied the dregs from his cup,
Shuffled back inside the house,
Sat down and began to write,
And he wrote of nothing but
Joy joy joy
Love
And loss loss loss
That moment of awareness is now forever lost.

VI.

That same old man looks out at you
And sings, crows, howls, and caws out
Joy joy joy
Love
And loss loss loss
This shared moment is now forever lost.

THE LOTUS

Body
Roots rest in the mud
Lovely blossom floats above
How slender the stem

Mind
The roots grip the mud
The blossom floats above
The slender stem sways

Soul
From the earth below
Beauty of the spirit flows
Fragrance floats on air

East to West
From the earth below
Beauty of the spirit flows
How fragrant the rose

The Practice
Life flows from matter
Through soul and spirit toward
Some more distant goal

WELL, IT'S ABOUT TIME
A Crown of Sonnets

I.

If one could stop time's impetuous flight
For an instant, a minute, or an hour,
Just long enough to hold it up to light,
Examine it with a microscope's power,

And break it down to its essential parts,
Is it reality that one would find?
Or would the yearnings of our untamed hearts
Confuse and then confound the searching mind?

As one turned this multifaceted gem
This way and that way in his shaking hand
Would love and truth and beauty come to him?
And if they did how could he understand?

One never knows until one takes the test
The searching mind will never be at rest.

II.

The searching mind will never be at rest,
Although there are wise men who make the claim
Emptiness lies at the end of the quest -
The emptiness from which creation came.

The quest begins with becoming aware
Of each precise moment of experience
Aware of what is and what is not there.
The first person singular, present tense.

The cultivation of the mind begins
With inundation of sensation.
The cultivation of the mind extends
To the cessation of sensation.

Who is it that's aware of being aware?
Is anyone home? Anyone still there?

III.

Is anyone home? Anyone still there?
This must be what it is like to be blest,
The answer to a contemplative's prayer,
To be at one with that great emptiness.

The first person singular disappears.
When there is no beautiful object left
It's beauty herself who will move you to tears.
Loss need not leave the lover bereft.

In the absence of the beloved one
Love herself will fill the aching heart.
The restless, searching mind at last has come
To the end of the quest. Now it must start

To live with this new found reality –
The unity of truth, love and beauty.

IV.

The unity of truth, love, and beauty
Does not buy groceries or pay the lease
Does not burden the seeker with a duty
To strive for justice, harmony, and peace.

The Buddha sneaked away in the dark night
Leaving behind mother, father, wife and child
To search for that ineffable insight,
Wandering, lost and alone, through the wild.

Christ was not there to comfort his mother
In her old age. It was not peace he brought,
But a sword between brother and brother.
Leave your family these holy men taught.

Must the search for that blessed selflessness
Always begin with acts of selfishness?

V.

Always begin with acts of selfishness.
No matter which path you choose to pursue
To seek the blinding light of emptiness,
Whether truth, beauty, or love calls to you,

It is you who must make the decisions,
You who must put reality to the test,
You who must make the endless revisions,
And must decide what's cursed, and what is blest.

Before one sees the beauty of the true,
Or knows the truth of the beautiful,
Or feels love for the beautifully true:
Truth and love springing from the beautiful;

From the confines of one's society
One must have the cool courage to break free.

VI.

One must have the cool courage to break free.
What are these ties that bind our minds and hearts?
They are formed by all we touch, hear, and see.
They form the whole of which we are the parts.

The softness of a mother's loving touch,
The firmness of a father's protecting strength,
The joy of breathing are almost too much.
But we become jaded with joy at length,

The miraculous becomes commonplace,
We lose our sense of life's awesome wonder.
The love of life now fades without a trace,
Lost in the roar of life's rolling thunder.

When life becomes too vivid, too intense,
Around our awareness we build a fence.

VII.

Around our awareness we build a fence,
To filter the onrush of perception
From an unintelligible nonsense
Into useful units of cognition.

The trembling leaves of trees shine in the sun,
Wild flowers waft their sent, bees buzz, birds sing,
Multicolored insects, fly, crawl, hop, run -
The six senses franticly processing,

Organizing, sequencing, separating,
Integrating the brain's line of defenses
To keep efficiently operating
In spite of the surfeit of the senses.

The mind sorts the chaos of perception
Into meaningful bits of information.

VIII.

Into meaningful bits of information
From which we construct our reality
Seeking salvation, fleeing damnation
Finding refuge in commonality.

Gestalts like beads on an unending string
Now, and now, and now, and now, unwinding
No time to think, no time to stop and bring
Attention to bear on the unending

Processing of the flow of perception
Into things we can name and control
Desperate for some kind of protection
Saying this is, and this is not, my soul.

Constructing a self, an identity,
From the plenitude of infinity.

IX.

From the plenitude of infinity
Striving to create a sense of order
Separating the startling complexity
Into what is me and what is the other.

This is my thumb and this must be my toe
The world disappears when I close my eyes
Sounds and shapes and colors come and then go
Each new boundary a complete surprise.

He is not all that he touches, sees, or hears.
Bits of this world belong to only him,
The other is the source of joys and fears.
The sense of unity fades and grows dim.

From the garden we are split asunder
To ease our fears we forfeit the wonder.

X.

To ease our fears we forfeit the wonder.
At first all we experience is magic.
When magic works for us no longer
To explain the unremitting tragic

Consequences of mundane existence
We place vengeful gods in the sky
And continue our stubborn insistence -
We will understand it all bye and bye

Building up layer after shielding layer
Of defenses to the terror of existence
Hoping to mitigate with praise and prayer
With sacrifice and repentance

The only universal certainty
Today we are, but one day we won't be.

XI.

Today we are, but one day we won't be.
Experience of common existence,
Movements through space, the pull of gravity,
Leave us with an overwhelming sense

Of separation and alienation
Of the despair that breeds nihilism..
Is there no chance of salvation?
No escape from this self-built prison?

Where do we turn to answer this question?
To the self-reports of other seekers
Who found, past all hope, a resolution.
We must turn to mankind's wisdom keepers.

When these wise ones reached the end of the line
They looked inside themselves. What did they find?

XII.

They looked inside themselves. What did they find?
They found the self to be an illusion
They found the source of their sorrow and pain
To be due to a needless confusion.

This hard won self-sufficient identity
That is so necessary for survival
Carries with it a heavy penalty.
Certain death, with no hope of revival.

The tragic story need not end there.
At the core of all mystic traditions
Is a path that leads away from despair,
But it is not free. There are conditions.

There are some rules and you must now learn them.
They are not hard. You have always known them.

XIII.

They are not hard. You have always known them:
Pay attention, be kind, and be honest.
Try to do good, and try not to do harm
Morality reduced to this short list.

Paying attention, that is the hard one,
All have the inclination to be kind,
Being honest is a habit hard won,
Good and harm can often seem entwined.

Yet there is a way out of the quandary,
A way to cut through all the confusion
A way that's open to all and sundry.
We must open again to life's profusion.

Each individual sensation is proof:
From the universe we are not aloof.

XIV.

From the universe we are not aloof.
The forces and particles that form stars
Form these magnificent bodies of ours.
Physicists and psychics proclaim this truth.

The body is at home here, so is the mind.
Evanescent beauty that moves to tears,
Truth that wakens, and then allays our fears,
Love greater than we ever thought we could find,

Lies all around us ready to our hand
We need only look, listen, smell or touch
To know what infinity has brought to pass:
Reality beyond what we comprehend,

Each sensation once again too much.
Eternity expressed in a blade of grass.

XV.

Eternity expressed in a blade of grass.
Led by the beauty of the manifest
We discover the truth of the unmanifest
Where only love can fill the emptiness

And lead us back into the bleak domain
Of uncertainty, doubt, and confusion.
Overwhelmed by suffering's profusion
We take up the duty there to remain.

And if one does his bit to ease the pain
And replace the false sense of alienation
With the knowledge of our integration,
When the soul can no longer stand the strain,

One could go softly into that good night
If one could stop time's impetuous flight

PINKSKY'S DEFINITION

I once heard the Poet Laureate
Of the whole United States say,
 "A poem is a column of air
Vibrating in someone's throat."
Then what are these smears of ink
Printed on processed pulp wood?
Are they mere ghosts of poems
Waiting for someone to breathe
Them back to life?

Perhaps it should be a crime
To tear a living poem from a throat
And entomb it in print.
Is a poetry anthology a graveyard
Of undead poems
Desperately seeking a living host?

I know I would not want
My final resting place to be
On page 493 of a Norton anthology.
Perhaps I needn't worry.

PART II

DEEP BLUE AND BLANK

Sky deep blue
And blank
But for the few fluffs
Of frothy white

Dust in the yard
Worn out tools
Forlorn heaps of rusted iron
Rotted wood

Stench of cow lot
Stench of pig pen

Milk bucket turned over fence post
Locusts' monotonous hum
Shimmering heat

Soft words quietly spoken
And all that ache of anger

WEEDS IN THE YARD

The children are grown and now there's no one home
There are weeds in the yard and the wheat ground's hard
But the redbuds still swell in the spring
And sometimes he can't help but sing
In a discordant howl of joy and pain
For the parched earth that longs for rain
The coyote hungry in the thicket
The cottontail anxious in the bunch grass
The monarchs driven on their epic journey
The geese that vee the skies
And bring unlooked for tears to his eyes
As the season turns and his heart burns
And all the sorrow of man rolls down the sky
In the splendor of the setting sun
When the cold remorseless stars appear
He traces the planets in their paths
And cuts another notch on his much scarred heart
To mark the passage of another year
And how eternity draws near

One day the stars will have another shape
As equinoxes precess and mankind seeks redress
For sins against the Mother, sins against the Father
Neglect of the Child and excess run wild
Envy of the Brother, hatred of the Sister
Denial of the Lover and the striping of Earth's cover

Will there always be enough milkweed
For the monarchs to feed as they float from south to north
Will the wild geese always find their marsh
Will the seasons continue to turn
Winter cold summer warm
In between the fall and spring
Will dark hair always fall
Over white shoulders
And the world be renewed
As it grows ever older

GNARLED TREE

On a small knoll
Overlooking a small lake
A short, gnarled tree
Is caught
In its last contortions

Petrified
In an agony
Of peeling bark

Its withered limbs
Reaching up
Into the sky
That has borne
It
Down

THE GAME FISH

Only the game fish
Swims up stream
But
When streams no longer run
When shallow stagnant pools
Lie stinking in the sun
The game fish is first
To turn his belly up
Flip his tail and lie still
Leaving the bog
To the bullhead
The crawdad and
The frog

NOSTALGIA

In the deep cool
                    of almost dark
chores done
                bath taken
                                supper cooking
nocturnal bird trill
                        hangs on air
in mind
            in ear
                    in memory

after images of sound
                                    defined
                                        in silence
splash of light
                    from kitchen door
smell of ham
                    in frying pan

cotton fields in full bloom
                                    fresh plowed wheat stubble
thump of dog tail
                    on door step
last faint after glow
                    in memory
                                    bird trill
birds t
            r
            i
              l
              l

SALLY GO ROUND

Sally go round the sun
Sally go round the moon
Sally go round the chimney pots
On a Saturday afternoon.

Grandma's in the pig pen
Grandpa's in the shed
Baby wants his supper
When the cows are fed.

Hound dog in the chicken run
Daughter on the town
Father oils the old shotgun
Mother sews the gown.

Full moon setting in the west
Rooster crowing hard
Preacher in his Sunday best
High Sheriff riding hard

Preacher picking out his text
Banker in the pew
Deacons meet on Tuesday next
Finances to review

If I'd as much money as I could tell
I never would cry old clothes to sell
Old clothes to sell
Old clothes to sell
I never would cry old clothes to sell

33

BRUTE FACT

The hide has not yet dried
Coyotes still feed on fetid intestines

The old cow could not quite get up
On the clear night when the wind fell
After the ice storm

The hills lay silent
As night eyes watched

A full moon rose as the temperature dropped

I cannot revel in the universal pleasantries
Or the more profound pedantries

Brute fact lies too close at hand

Cold and pain and freezing rain
Followed by the clear cold night
And the circle of unblinking eyes

These I know and
In part
Understand

THE MEANING

"What does it mean?" said Reader to Writer.
"It's just the Word becoming flesh again,
Passing through your eyes and into your brain,
Spirit finding its way into matter."

"Oh, I thought perhaps the old brindle cow
The herd had abandoned and left behind
Was a symbol for suffering mankind,
And that the cold and the dark were somehow

Symbolic of society's indifference."
"Yes, of course, that is what I had in mind,
I just did not know it was at the time.
I must have been in some kind of a trance

Where cold is just cold, dark just dark somehow,
And an old brindle cow, just an old cow."

35

DANCING WITH DEMONS

Electricity crackling in the crinkled brain
Sights and sounds that will not come again

Once you've danced with demons
And argued with angels
And conspired with a lover
To catch a soul from the air

Once you've seen the burning bush
And walked upon the water

The spirit grows weary of the flesh
The flesh no longer cares to atone
For spirit's distrust of the bone

The eye loses its sparkle
The hair loses its luster
The mind loses it focus

The soul grows tired of the earth
And longs for another birth

SIXTEEN LINES

I thought I might write sixteen lines
Of iambic tetrameter,
To limit my thought and to confine
My tendency to meander.

To add even more discipline,
I thought I might add rhyme to meter.
To this evolving paradigm
I now must add subject matter.

To be worthy of the effort
Of the reader and the writer
It must ring true and not distort
The thought to better fit the meter.

I should compose a sound retort
To those who cannot find the time
To shape their thought in lines that rhyme
And find free verse a last resort.

COMMON GROUND

Young folk can find inspiration
In love, death and indignation.
Old folk look to those same deep wells
When their story they wish to tell.

The young find death a tragedy
And look to love for salvation.
The old find love a tragedy
And look to death for salvation.

Both young and old find righteous rage
An easy way to fill a page.
Sensitive to societies'
Arbitrary inequities,

They make sure that we understand
That there should be a better plan.

PART III

NAÏVE REALISM

Extend a point and it becomes a line.
Extend a line and it becomes a plane.
Extended planes become solid things,
Yet still they are only something ideal,
Beyond the reach of touch or taste or feel.
Their only existence is in the mind
Unless they can find duration in time.
Are things that exist only in the mind
Any less real? Or real in some other way?

Today, at 4:30 in the afternoon, I decided to save the world
by writing poetry and reading philosophy. Everyone can
relax now. I'm on the job.

TO BE

I
I am
I am that
I am that I
I am that I am
I am that, I am that, I am that, I am that
I am that I am
I am that
I am
I

First person singular
Unique individual
A corporeal biological entity
A complex self-replicating dynamic system
Very far from equilibrium
Dependent on the environment to furnish air,
To furnish water,
To furnish nutrients to maintain
These two trillion cells that are bounded by my skin.

I, first person, singular
An awareness, a consciousness
A unique product of a few billion years of evolution
Unique and singular in genetic composition and epigenetic
expression
Unique and singular in memories and life experiences

I, a stranger and afraid, in a world I never made
I, isolated and vulnerable, needy, longing for security
In constant danger of losing that first person singularity

MOCK DRAMATIC DOGGEREL IN SONNET FORM

"I just finished one more awesome sonnet!"
"Oh, did you now? A sonnet? Are you sure?"
"Of course I'm sure, bet my life upon it!
It's a sonnet for sure, correct and pure."

"Before you place such a heavy wager
Maybe we should take into consideration,
Taking your sweet time and at your leisure,
Some particulars of composition."

"It has ten syllables in every line,
Three quatrains and a final rhymed couplet
And that makes it a sonnet, friend of mine."
"Fine lines and rhymes are not a sonnet yet.

Is it lyrical? Does it have a turn?
Silly man. It seems you will never learn."

43

POTENTIAL

At first there was nothing, nothing at all.
Yet deep in that nothing potential slept.
A potential so vast that when expressed
It became an infinitesimal point
Of energy containing all that now is
And all that will ever come to be.
The bubble of nothing burst into being
Infinitely hot, infinitely bright
Infinitely dense but expanding
Unfurling, uncurling, cooling
Time and space extending their place

We now know we live on a big blue ball
Spinning through a far from empty space
Rotating some twenty-four thousand miles
Each and every twenty-four hours
Day chasing night away from east to west
As we rise up to work or lie down to rest
The horizon falling away to reveal
And then rising up to conceal - the sun

This slightly tilted spinning blue sphere
Is sweeping out around an inferno
At sixty-six thousand six hundred and sixty miles per hour
The solar system is racing around the galaxy
The galaxy is rushing from somewhere
To somewhere else as though it has
Somewhere else it needs to be
And yet we have the illusion of sitting still
Of leaving and returning to the same place
As though the earth sits still at the center
While the universe performs its cartwheels

On this slightly tilted spinning blue sphere
Bathed in radiation from the sun
Shielded by a benevolent atmosphere
Matter has humped itself up into heaps
That can maintain themselves and replicate themselves,
And some of these self-replicating heaps
Are aware of being aware.

To maintain themselves in space and through time
These self-organizing, self-replicating heaps
Must consume matter and dissipate energy.

The great dance - energy generating matter
Matter generating energy
The one giving rise to the many
The many giving rise to the one
And everything that arises is at once
A thing in itself and a part of a larger thing
And that larger thing is itself a thing
And a part of a larger thing
From particle to atom to molecule to compound
To planet to solar system to galaxy
To clusters of galaxies to a universe
And from a universe to something I know not what
And all from a bubble of potential that burst
Into being a few hundreds of billions of years ago

And if some of these groups of things
Following the laws of physics and chemistry
Have learned to maintain and replicate
Across time and space and some of these
Energy-consuming and energy dissipating

Systems are so complexly organized that
They can perceive the world around them
And are aware of their own mortality
Then why not take joy in the dance
That first placed us in and then made us aware
Of our circumstance.

ACROSTIC

As a way to pass the time
Counting words that
Rhyme is a rather
Old fashioned occupation of
Septuagenarian poets
Trying to
Incite the muse to
Choose them one more time

BEATITUDE

Blessed be
Each
Aching
Trembling
Iteration
That
Unfolds
Dancing
Exultantly

AWARE

Always
Watching
Alert
Resilient
Existence

47

EQUANIMITY

Ease
Quiet
Ubiquitous
Anonymous
Non-striving
Instantaneous
Mitigation of
Ignorance's
Timeless
Yearning

RETURNING

Retracing
Each
Twisting
Undulating
Road
Neatly
Imitating
Nostalgia's
Ghosts

AGAINST THE FLOW

A strong current in the main stream
Creates eddies on the margins,
Little vortexes moving slow
Working their way against the flow
Particles constantly changing
Yet the turbulence still remaining
A dynamic natural system
Quite far from equilibrium

ON THE BUS RIDE

The cars, the endless lines of cars, four lanes, eight lanes,
twelve lanes, clover-leaf stacked above over-pass panic
despair exit left exit right bumper to bumper stop and go
must get out of the city must find some place quiet
pavement holding the heat one passenger per car, I 30 west,
I 20 east the mark of the beast fumes in the air trash on the
ground Honda Lexus Chevy Hummer 18-wheeler hauling
pretzels hauling Pepsi hauling pipe hauling cattle nothing in
its right place everything moving everything in process
everything in flux electrons spitting out of the heart of the
sun all fore-ordained since the big bang drill the seas drill
the arctic drill the desert more cars more suburban mansions
fell the forests grind the limestone lay down more asphalt
raise the speed limit make more highways make bigger
trucks haul in more stuff move farther out in the country till
one day we hit the wall till one day the lights don't come on
till one day there's no gas at the station till one day the
nanny doesn't show up till one day the school bus doesn't
run till one day the tall buildings fall down till one day no
one comes when the city drowns till one by one the pizza
parlors close till one by one the shelves of the super market
go empty till the banks close their doors we'll watch on TV
while looters ransack the stores while rioters raid the police
station while Air Force One takes off for a destination
unknown no I don't want you to do anything it's already too
late it's been too late for a while the top soil is gone the
forests are gone the rivers are foul the ocean is foul the
ozone layer is gone the temperature of the earth has risen
your 401K won't save you your stock portfolio won't save
you your gated community won't save you your shot gun
won't save you your cell phone won't save you your low-
carb diet won't save you Jesus Christ wouldn't save you
even if He could...

50

GLASS DOORS

A squat heavy ugly woman
Franticly guarding
Two large grocery bags
Of baggage
Periodically leans against
Glass doors that will not open
Opens her mouth and adds
To the already slimy floor

BLACK BASTARD
GIT AWAY FROM ME
BLACK BASTARD

While a short boyman
Whose knees sag towards each other
Wonders up and down
In front of glass doors
That will not open
And he is holding the arm
Of an unbelievably
Wizened wrinkled woman
Who might be thirty-five
And might be sixty-five
Another woman comes
And joins them and she is
Even uglier and more wrinkled
Than the other woman and
All three of them push
On the glass doors that will not open
The boyman starts whimpering
And people look at their tickets
And tell them gate 22
But they are in between gate 2 and gate 10
There is a line at gate 10

And you are in the line at gate 10

A tall thin Negro youth
Is staring at you
His eyes
Slits
And you look at him
A long time and then
You have to look away

The crippled boyman is keening
Their bus is about to leave gate 22
And they cannot find gate 22

The squat woman is still spitting
And shouting

BLACK BASTARDS
THE BLACK BASTARDS
KIN GIT THROUGH THE DOORS
ANY TIME THEY WANT

The whole place stinks
You cannot shut out the stink
You cannot forget the youth
Still staring at you
People are jammed all around you

THE BUS
WHERE KIN WE GIT ON THE BUS
STAY AWAY FROM ME
BLACK BASTARD

Silent unblinking stare
Stink
And glass doors that will not open

St. Louis bus station 5 A.M. 1972

INVOCATION

Let not our souls from freedom hide
Nor in anger seek to abide
But seek to find some better thing
To set the bird upon the wing
And bring to light the golden store
Still hidden at the gleaming core
Beneath the public impiety
Of our weary society

Sacred images still arise
Out of our sleep, behind our eyes.
The eternal ones are still at home,
In the blood and beneath the bone.
We can still call to them in rhyme
And attempt to redeem the time
By tuning the strings of our hearts
To the scale of the ancient arts.

The world has been at pains to shape
That long, slender, shapely nape.
The blood which flushes that fair cheek,
An admonishment to the meek,
Makes immortal the souls of man,
And, for those who can understand,
Explains the arcane mystery
Of why god wills for us to be.

THE SAND IN THE WHORL

Losing is no reason to surrender
The cause still needs someone to defend her
There's always the recourse to outlawry
To poverty and demagoguery
To subterfuge and subversion
Until the bile rises in aversion
Looking back from this narrow place
To a time when we still walked in grace

The grain of sand caught in the whorl
If held onto, becomes the pearl.

A PASSION FOR RHYME

A palsied old man with a passion for rhyme
The singing of sparrows in the evening time
The twisting of the moon as the seasons shift
And other shards found in the alluvial rift

Oh, the tunes that spring from those full lips
The souls crying out to be born
Spirit longing for flesh in her dark ringlets
And Dylan Thomas quiet in the dark night

The wind wears ever at the ledges
Of hills that rise in waves of hardened bone
Gramma grass rooted in lichens legacy
And star dust in the cracks of the stone

Coyote and bob-cat, wolf and mountain lion
Grey eagle and hawk, owl and chaparral
Look down from the hills
And long for something soft to kill

55

SAYING YES TO NO

Because every no implies a yes
And every yes contains a demand
And every object is a metaphor
Beyond our command
In emptiness we must seek our bliss

Working toward affirmation
Working through abnegation
Finding a reason for a joyous season
Courage in the face of ego's death
And shortness of breath
Seeking a source for courage
Beyond mere outrage

The swallows came back again this year
The hills are home to the spotted deer
The geese and the ducks have come
And are mostly gone

There is strength in the soil
Strength in the sun
The killdeer and meadowlark are in the grass
But this year or next may be the last

Man needs to work towards a graceful demise
Find a way to leave the world intact as he fades
Joyously embracing his diminishment
An affirmation of his limitations

That the streams may run clear again
That the breeze may blow clean again

WHAT WILL BE

When some sweet-souled singer sings
Remembered beauty of forgotten dreams
A myth will grow and a mystery
To show what has been
And shape what will be

The slow-fading twilight
    Reveals the silver moon
       And down the deep-starred
             Stairway of sky
                Comes night

CLOTHING THE EMPTINESS
"He do the police in different voices."
(Draft title for T.S. Eliot's _The Wasteland_)

Pulling words around me lest the cold get in
Wrapping concepts and memories about me
Clothing the emptiness.

I am the one who pulled a long white sack
Between meager rows of dry land cotton
In this very field.
 (Others pulled sacks in this same field.
That is not who you are.)

I am one of the few who realize
That all actions have unintended consequences
And that inaction has its unintended consequences.
(You stole that from the old Lama in Kipling's "Kim."
That's not who you are.
You can do better than that.)

When I came up to bat on softball diamonds
From Ft. Cobb to Anadarko, from Binger to Cache,
The catcher from the other team would wave
The outfielders deeper and around to right.
(How long ago was that?
How many times did that really happen?
You're not even trying now.)

Okay. It was me sitting
In the fork of a tree
Reading Camus
By the edge of the lagoon
In front of the art museum
In Cleveland, Ohio
On a warm spring day in 1964

58

When a slender, long-haired, green-eyed girl
Called out, "You come down from there."
(So that's who you are;
A young man in a tree, reading Camus?
You keep telling me who
You might have been.
But, who are you?)

I am the one sitting here,
Now,
Trying to find out who I am.
(Not having much luck, are you?)

Okay, smart guy, who are you?
(Illegal question.)

PART III

OKLAHOMA POEMS

If I were to write Oklahoma poems I would be sure to mention the monarch butterfly....use her for a symbol of some kind, how her erratic fluttering gets her from a home she will never know again to a home she has never known. I would use the migration of the Great Canadian Goose as a metaphor for something beautiful, periodic and recurrent. I would not leave out Old Man Coyote, trickster and scavenger, and his influence on politics and business. Of course you must use the unrelenting wind and the heat and the cold, the dust storms, the blue northers, the tornadoes....and do it in the rhythm and inflection that Bob Dylan picked up from Woody Guthrie and exaggerated. That's enough to start with.

CAN'T DANCE, TOO WET TO PLOW

Rain falling on the old Slick Hills tonight
Winter wheat up and covering the ground
Barley just barely sown before the rain
Maize too green to cut before the first frost
Too muddy to cut firewood and besides
The chimney is full of bird nests
So it looks like I have nothing to do
But sit and write pentameter for you

Sometimes I think when it rains in the hills
And water runs from the rocks in rills
Bluegrass dull bronzing in the fading light
That those who hold positions of power
And measure their time by the quarter hour
Should come and sit and be quiet
As rain falls on the old Slick Hills tonight

RAINY DAY

Low clouds lie upon the slick hills
Brown puddles in the gravel drive
Chickens huddle under the pick-up truck

Rainy, lazy, down-home day
Time to rest, to think, to gather
Spirit and strength

To live the life that is simple
And pure as a flame

Consuming and consumed
Consistently and constantly
Wax and wane flickering flame
Cast light and shadow

A life without superfluity
A life of simple joys and pains

Hot food on a cold day
A cold drink in the summer sun
Rain after drought
Water in the Spring

Seeds slow swelling and bursting
Tentative tendrils above the hardening crust
Slow uncurling of dicotyledons under the sun
Energy being converted into matter

GATHERING DUSK

Now that I have heard the sparrows sing
The rites of spring and endured
Summer's litany of dusky doves
And witnessed the full liturgy
Of autumn, I hear other bells
Call to other ceremonies.

The riotous song birds of April
Strut and dance
Defend their territory
And attract their fates.

All that lilting song,
The figures cut in air,
The loops and swirls end
In pairs and the desire
To build and fill a nest.

When the nest is empty
And summer's flowers fade,
The song birds forget to sing.
The pairs seek out other company.

A flock begins to form.
They fly about in unison,
Filled with an overpowering
Vision of a distant landscape
Where flowers still bloom and birds
Sing in the gathering dusk
Of warm late afternoons.

UNCLEAN

Strange that the symptoms show
So slowly and so late.
Take them to the priest and
If the red shows within the white,
They are unclean,
And their habitation shall be
Without the camp.

Yea, but if the priest himself
Be stricken
Who shall make the pronouncement?

Yea, and when the camp
Is a beleaguered fortress
With the unclean host
Raging without the walls,
Will you send your finest and best
To the unclean host?

SMALL TOWN SATURDAY NIGHT

Wandering
Among deep pools of evening,
I heard a dying elm
Call my name.

Splendors
Of the apocalypse
Were falling down the sky
Like rain.

No one seemed to notice.
They lounged around
Back yard barbeques
In their underwear.

I heard Salome laughing,
Saying she didn't care,
Or maybe she said something
About a ribbon for her hair.

It kept me awake all night,
I can tell you that.
Well, that and the rat
That gnawed on my collar bone
As I lay under the stars
All alone.

TIME TO GO IN

The lion in the yard
Can be dangerous.
He gives no warning when
The predatory instinct kicks in.
The leopard is less worrisome,
Especially when she's been well fed.

Old lion, he sometimes kills just for fun.
Maybe we better go in now.
It's getting dark
And barbarians
Are coming down the drive.

WE LOST

We lost the war and the other side
Now controls the history book

Few remember our stubborn pride
Or the losses that we took
In the face of the enterprise
That desecrated this holy space

Few refuse to compromise
And bargain from their place
At the trough where the big eaters feed
On the entrails of the world

While the earth's mothers bleed
And the abomination is whirled
High over the heads of the multitude
Mired in the mud streets of their pain

I wish we had the fortitude
To take up the impossible task again
To risk it all and lose it all once more
To put a foot in the slamming door

DENIAL

The Mocking Bird trills
Expressing his will
Defining his space
In bursts of song
In late summer moonlight he sings
From the depths of his soul
At the top of the tree
Filling the night with the ancient song

The cow calved in early spring
She stands in the bunch grass
Knees locked eyes glazed
Calf curled in the grass nearby
Not aware of the changes winter may bring
She drinks in the moonlight
The bird song
The occasional call of the coyote
In the dark of the night
The calf stirs in the grass
She reaches down
And comforts it with her tongue

71

FORK IN THE ROAD

Two thoughts entangled in a mellow mood
Sorry I could not follow both
I soon began to fret and brood
Troubled, unsure, misunderstood
To abandon either, I was loath

I wanted to choose a thought so profound
One so well-ordered no one could claim
It trivial, mundane, or unsound.
A thought that could hit a wall and rebound
If only I could choose and ease the strain

But the two thoughts were so entwined
I was still uncertain, still unsure
Then my mind became clear and refined
The proper thought could be easily defined
I, I thought the thought more obscure

WAVE RIDER'S WIFE

The waves which wander the watery world
Howl their pain when on harsh stone hurled.
The wind which harries them on to their bane
Carries the roar and rage of the wild rampage
Far inland where it weakens, grows small,
And whimpers round an earthen wall

A grey gull in a grey sky
Utters his cry into the wind
Banks and turns back to the breakers roar
Leaving behind the oaken door
From which a woman weary with waiting
Hears the wild waters watches the grey gull.

Melancholy grey of gull and sky
Fills her waiting watchful eye.
The distant breakers rhythmic roar
The lonesome cry of a gull passing by
Weave and work within her brain
Forming the warp for the woof of her pain.

THE CYCLE

A little wriggly form, in unlovely muck born,
Dreams of air and sky and vows of one day to fly.
Life is easy, food sure in his pile of manure,
Yet he knows he must dare to try to fly in air.

From this pitiable worm comes a much finer form
Traveling far and near in the sky blue and clear.
But still he is not free, nor will he ever be
From that unlovely dung he wallowed in when young.

There he returns again in sorrow and in pain.
It is there he must feed. It is there he must breed,
And, when his young is born, a little wriggly form
In muck and dung will lie and dream of air and sky.

TEMPTATION

Tempted to turn again to anger
To drink once more from that trusted
Source of passion and inspiration
To rage and rail, condemn and blame
To feel once more the strength
Of righteous indignation
Bound by a vow of affirmation
I shall not turn again to negation
But stumble through this wasted land
Seeking for the sources of joy
Longing for the blessings of equanimity

STRANGE LOOP

I seem to have lost interest
In trying to say what can be said
And in trying to say what can't be said

But have become fascinated
By the sinuous coiling and uncoiling
Of trying to unsay that which can't be said.

The universe is not unitary
Its manifold manifestations collapse
Into the teeming emptiness of the unmanifest,

Neither creating nor destroying
Giving birth nor dying

Emptiness expressing its eternal non-essence
In the temporal manifest
Having no essence save its expression
Of non-essence

I
I am
I am that
I am that I
I am that I am that I am that I am that I am
I am that I
I am that
I am
I

THE WAXING AND THE WANING

In the chill October mornings
Crows caw from across cool fields of fall
Crickets sadly mark the passing moments
And summers bright burning children
Feel the turning of the year

Butterflies forlornly ride northern breezes
Floating toward their rendezvous
To spawn the race that will
Ride the south winds
When the sun returns

Migrant splashes of brilliant color
Drifting south on gossamer wings
Burning bright the child of summer sings

He was too old to die so young
His dreams undreamed his songs unsung
His body scattered beneath a declining sun

Unmourned by maiden, wife, or mother
His body now lies in the market place
But once a lover loved this ruined face

When the bright ones were winging north
On damp winds that smelled of rain
He sang a wild and jumbled song
But his shadow lengthened and his song waned
Once they decked his brow with wild flowers
And shouted as he raced through the town
But his shadow raced along side
Biding its time
Whispering in his ear
Waiting for the waning of the year

IT WAS IN ALL THE PAPERS

How can you write a poem that's not about the war?

Although electrons may spin in two directions at the same
time
And we don't know if the cat in the box is alive or dead
Until we look
Metal projectiles still tear flesh
Blood is still necessary to life

How can you write a poem that's not about the war?

Humming birds drink nectar from the honeysuckle
Quail call to one another in the tall grass
The cow suckles her calf on the warm hillside
But trinitrotoluene still expands rapidly
Giving off heat which strips flesh from the bones

How can you write a poem that's not about the war?

There is a slender maiden dancing on the lawn
She is the reason the sun rises
And is the rising sun itself
A machine gunner has her in his sights

How can you write a poem that's not about the war?

HIDDEN HOPE

The wind that whistles over this low hill,
The chill that settles into the marrow
Numbs the brain and stifles the will
That would be thinking about tomorrow.

The frozen earth, the bare, ice-covered trees
Rattling in the rush of frigid air,
What inspiration can be caught from these?
What can save us from this blank despair?

When the empty howling universe
Only mirrors the emptiness within,
And we are unable to bless or curse,
The sap is low and the blood runs thin.

Entwined in a ball, far underground,
Rattlesnakes wait for spring to come round.

PART IV

AMAZED BY GRACE

As a child I was amazed by grace
I wandered in the garden
With the dew still on the roses
Leaning on the ever-lasting arms
Safe and secure from all alarms
Knowing that some glad day I would
Fly away for this old world was not
My home I was just a-passing through
I was pressing on that upward way
New heights a-gaining every day
Onward with the Christian soldiers
Marching as to war with the cross
Of Jesus going on before
I cherished the old rugged cross
That stood on a hill lone and gray
I was sure that Jesus loved me
Because the bible told me so
Just as I was without one plea
Just as I was and waiting not
To rid my soul of one dark blot
I was saved saved saved
My little ten year old soul
That had not yet discovered
An original sin
Was dunked in the cold spring water
Of Taha Creek I was redeemed
Halleluiah Thine the glory
Halleluiah amen
And the rhythms and rhymes of those
Old Baptist hymns will always beat
In my mind and inform my art

ADVICE TO YOUNG POETS

Do not compromise your arrogance
By reading too much good poetry.

If you want to tunnel into mythology
And mine the rich deposits
Discovered by Jung and Campbell
For god's sake don't read Yeats and Graves.

They've been down those shafts before you.
Do you think you will delve as deep
Or report your findings as well?

Protect your ignorance
Maintain your arrogance
And you may discover a unique stance.

If you want to explore
The mysteries of consciousness
And its relations to spirit and matter
Don't read too widely.

Leave Rumi and the Sufis alone.
Stay away from Lao Tzu and the Daoists.
Shun Pater, Hopkins and Eliot.
Do not bother with St. John of the Cross
And all those other mystics.
They would only confuse and discourage you.

Let your innocence protect your audacity.

ABOUT AVERAGE

man the mean
                ing
                        less
                                mass

man the so
            phis
                    ticated so
cial an(i)mal
                mean
                        ing
                                less
                                        than so

cial in
        sects in
                stinc
                        tive
                                ly
completing their com
                        pli
                                cated
                                        tasks
                                                mean
                                                        ing
                                                                less

abstruse ab
            (sub) stractions
having no
            thing
                        to do
with any living
                        struggling
                                    l
                                        o
                                            v
                                                i
                                                    n
                                                    g
                        man thing

GWENDOLYN BROOKS VISITS THE UNITARIAN DISCUSSION GROUP
"Ain't we cool?" from _The Pool Shooters_"

Ain't we cute
Ain't we sincere
Ain't we got existential despair
Don't we hate the war
Don't we feel sorry for the poor
We been to the holy lands
Israel and Tibet
We got there in a big old jet
We sorry bout the environment
Something should be done by the government
What's the best restaurant in Cancoon
We going down there sometime soon
We sensitive to other people's pain
We vacation in Southern Spain
We read the bible and the I Ching
We love Lao Tzu and Buddha and everything
We got central heat shag carpet and three cars
We never drink in red neck bars

US

You and I
        are boats afloat
                on the ocean of story
You and I
        are snapping turtles sunning
                on the logs of tradition
Spies from paradise
            You and I
                Awaiting rendition
We are the profits
        being reinvested
                into infrastructure
                    You and I
Consummate
        consumers
                of experience

Swimmers
        in the seas
                of phenomenon
You and I
        are high
                On the waters of life
Singers
        of the one song
                that can't be sung
Implications
        of the implicate order
                refugees from salvation
You
        and
           I

TRANING WHILE IT'S RAINING

thunder storm up the hill up the hill airborne air borne
can't stop won't stop airborne airborne airborne ranger
Ft. Polk summertime 20 mile march 40 pound pack 8 pound
M1 a1 rifle double time double time airborne airborne
airborne ranger you had a good home but you left your right
you left your left right left down the line the order came put
on your ponchos in the rain sound off one two sound off
three four bring it on down one two three four one
two....three four your left your left your left right left ain't
no use in looking down ain't no discharge on the ground
sound off one two sound off three four bring it on down one
two three four one two...three four your left your left your
left right left 90 degrees 100 per cent humidity rain beating
on steel pot and plastic poncho no place for body heat or
sweat to go one way one way up the hill up the hill one way
all the way can't stop won't stop a dull thump and a rattle
of steel pot and rifle as the first man went down you had a
good home but you left your right your left your right you
left up the hill up the hill combat boots sucking mud thump
thump two more men down hospital truck trailing the
platoon picking them up as they went down one way all the
way can't stop won't stop airborne airborne airborne ranger
the rain stopped the sun came out still we marched on with
those dammed ponchos on still men fell out from
dehydration and heat exhaustion Company halt stow your
ponchos fall out stack arms at ease water break smoke em if
you have em Surprisingly there were over half of us left
standing.

CONTENT

Poetry consists of
Observation
Self-revelation
Confession
And confabulation

With the tacit assumptions
That the universal is revealed
In the particular

And that the subjective
Has an objective correlative

And that we have the urge to create
A shared reality

And that words somehow
Someway
Convey meaning

WALK SLOWLY

Walk slowly through the tall grass
In the springtime
When the butterflies float
And the mockingbird sings.

Walk slowly through the springtime
When the coyote pups are newborn
and the swallows are building new nests.

If you walk too fast you might miss
The blossoms of the blue-eyed grass
And the false dandelions.

You might miss a turkey buzzard
Floating high overhead.

You might also find that old man rattlesnake
Has crawled out of his den.

He doesn't want to talk to you about an apple.
He's not busy being a symbol of immortality.
He just wants to break his long winter fast and
He does not want to be bothered.

ELLIS ISLAND – CHRISTMAS EVE

The wind which follows me
    Has swept across the sea
        And the waves beat on the shore

I've come a dreary ways
    In the dying of the days
        To stand before a narrow door

The wind carries the cries
    Of gulls that fill the skies
        And they speak to me of home

In the dying of the year
    When all is sad and drear
        Will I be left here all alone

The tide is at the neap
    The little rains do weep
        My heart is sore within my breast

I stand here all alone
    I must not think of home
        But keep my face turned to the west

Fear hate and poverty
    Drove me across the sea
        In search of hope in a new land

In quarantine I lay
    I may be turned away
        And denied this place to stand

On such a Christmas night
    Mother Mary brought forth the light
        To brighten a dark and dreary world

So I must hope and pray
    That with the coming day
        The sun will break through the cloud

Christ in mercy look down
    Keep soul and body sound
        Help me pass to the other side

And with the coming day
    May sorrows pass away
        And that narrow door open wide

NOT ALONE

As his father lay dying
The mourning doves crying
The crows all flew away
In the bone chilling gray
Of having nothing to say
He wasn't even trying

Infinite variation, pulsing sensation
Purple yellow and green
In shades never before seen
Lit up his inner screen
Unsought for consolation

The gray goose has found his home,
Though flesh sags on the bone
The moon still lights the night
Spirit rises above fright
And turns towards the light
None of us are alone

OLD MAN'S MAUNDERING

Wandering,
lost and alone,
standing in the rain
soaked to the bone,
Star crossed and cursed
refusing the best,
accepting the worst.

Land I farmed and houses I framed
are standing open to the driving rain.
Some battles I've fought,
some battles I've won
but mostly I've been on the run.

I've kept my head down.
I've run for cover,
but never did I abandon a lover.

All that I've done will be undone,
yet I will stand ashamed
before no one.

VILLANELLES

The highly structured villanelle is a nineteen-line poem with two repeating rhymes and two refrains. The form is made up of five tercets followed by a quatrain. The first and third lines of the opening tercet are repeated alternately in the last lines of the succeeding stanzas; then in the final stanza, the refrain serves as the poem's two concluding lines.

THE WINE I TASTED

I thought my life was wasted
Omission was my sin
I left the wine untasted

My strength I left untested
Neither all out nor all in
I thought my life was wasted

I left the foe unbested
Afraid to lose afraid to win
I left the wine untasted

Development arrested
The grain left in the bin
I thought my life was wasted

In the sheath my blade rested
Sharp edge kept safely in
I left the wine untasted

But now my wave has crested
I push the chips all in
Not all my life was wasted
At last the wine I've tasted

TO PASS THE TIME AWAY

I thought to write a villanelle
Upon a warm and cloudless day,
The reason why I cannot tell

There was no tale I had to tell.
'Twas just to pass the time away,
I thought to write a villanelle.

A restless mind I thought to quell.
With lines and rhymes I sought to play,
The reason why I cannot tell

Maybe I thought it would be swell
To tell a friend at close of day,
"I thought to write a villanelle."

A sad story to you I tell
About that warm and cloudless day,
The reason why I cannot tell.

Upon my friend the burden fell
To turn to me at last and say,
"You thought to write a villanelle?
The reason why I cannot tell!"

QUANTUM MAN

There is a quantum man named Sam. He is a cloud of virtual
personalities. He collapses into reality depending on where
and how and when you expect him to be. He may be a
particle and slam into your consciousness and he may just
be a wave as he passes by. You see, it's all in what the
observer expects. Sometimes he goes through mirrors,
sometimes he bounces off, and when nobody is watching he
just disappears. He can go through two different doors at the
same time. He can be here and there at the same time and he
takes all possible routes to get there.

ODE TO FORM

Three days have passed since last I cudgeled my brain
Into sullen, reluctant submission
To undergo the stress, to endure the strain,
Of disciplined poetic composition.

Three times around the earth has spun the sun,
 Moon, and stars into and out of the sky
Since last I sought to find a shape for thought.
To rectify this onerous omission,
I vow not to let another go by
Leaving that battle of wills still unfought.

97

BLESSED BE

Neither an unlikely accident
Nor a blessed miracle
This precious evanescent earth
Teeming with life
Humming with consciousness
But the expression of the unalterable
Laws of the universe

Blessed be the mystery of gravity
Blessed be the arcane sources
Of the weak and the strong forces
Blessed be the chrism of electro-magnetism
Blessed be the encoded information
That consistently defeats entropy
Blessed be   blessed be   blessed be

AGNOSTICS LAMENT

Sometimes it's hard
To keep from feeling gratitude
To resist the longing
For Someone or Something
To thank
For all the unlikely
Chance combinations
That led to the trillion cells
Enclosed in this skin
Having consciousness
And consciousness
Of that consciousness

98

EXTRAVAGANZAS

Having been bitten by Frost
Until my toes were cold and
Water dripped from my nose

I turned to the mystic fires
Of Yeats, but found that even
Mystic fires sometimes abate,

So I turned in confusion,
Not hoping to turn again,
To Eliot's elusive allusions,
To salvation and sin.

Wearied of walking the tight-rope
From not quite despair
To not quite hope

I sought out the firm stanzas
And elegant tempos
Of Wallace Stevens' extravaganzas.

.

ANOTHER SONNET

"I cannot write another damn sonnet.
They are stilted, they are stiff, they are trite
Not to put too fine a point upon it,
Another sonnet I refuse to write."

"A form so eloquent and so refined
And in these times, a form so neglected,
A form so complex yet so well defined,
How can its call ever be rejected?"

"Contriving rhymes at the end of each line,
Counting syllables till you are insane,
Is that your idea of a grand old time?
From this exercise I choose to refrain."

"Suit yourself my irresolute old friend,
This conversation has now come to an end."

ABOUT THE AUTHOR

Sam McMichael is a professional story-teller, a retired farmer-rancher, a long-time frequenter of open mic poetry venues and a lay Unitarian preacher. He lives on a small ranch in Southwestern Oklahoma with his artist wife, Terree, and his Airedale dog, Tessa.

Made in the USA
Lexington, KY
21 January 2017